UNLOCKING POTENTIAL

MASTER THE LAWS OF LEADERSHIP

BY SMART READS

Free Audiobook

As a thank you for being a Smart Reader you can choose 2 FREE audiobooks from audible.com. Simply sign up for free by visiting www.audibletrial.com/Travis to get your books.

Visit:
www.smartreads.co/freebooks
to receive Smart Reads books for FREE

Check us out on Instagram:
www.instagram.com/smart_readers
@smart_readers

ABOUT SMARTREADS

Choose Smart Reads and get smart every time. Smart Reads sorts through all the best content and condenses the most helpful information into easily digestible chunks.

We design our books to be short, easy to read and highly informative. Leaving you with maximum understanding in the least amount of time.

Smart Reads aims to accelerate the spread of quality information so we've taken the copyright off everything we publish and donate our material directly to the public domain. You can read our uncopyright below.

We believe in paying it forward and donate 5% of our net sales to Pencils of Promise to build schools, train teachers and support child education.

To limit our footprint and restore forests around the globe we are planting a tree for every 10 hardcover books we sell.

Thanks for choosing Smart Reads and helping us help the planet.

Sincerely,

Travis & the Smart Reads Team

Uncopyright 2017 by Smart Reads. No rights reserved worldwide. Any part of this publication may be reproduced or transmitted in any form without the prior written consent of the publisher.

Disclaimer: The publisher and author make no representations or warranties with respect to the accuracy or completeness of these contents and disclaim all warranties for a particular purpose. The author or publisher is not responsible for how you use this information. The fact that an individual or organization is referred to in this document as a citation or source of information does not imply that the author or publisher endorses the information that the individual or organization provided.

TABLE OF CONTENTS

Introduction	2
Chapter 1: What Leadership Is and What It Isn't	4
Chapter 2: Is Leadership Right For You?	13
Chapter 3: Approaching a New Role in Leadership	18
Chapter 4: Building Leadership Skills in the Workplace	28
Chapter 5: Leadership Styles	43
Conclusion	51
Smart Reads Vision	54

INTRODUCTION

How does one go about defining leadership? It is such a broad term that many people find it difficult to pinpoint exactly what it means for them at any given moment. It is a skill that applies itself in different ways for people in different leadership positions. The CEO of a major company needs to have a different style and command of leadership than a high school soccer coach. Not every leadership title calls for the firm, exacting instruction of a military general. Furthermore, we are often placed in positions of leadership without even knowing it. We find ourselves suddenly called upon to make a decision or to encourage a friend who reaches out in need of help. These too are critical leadership positions; in fact, the ways in which we are suddenly called to lead are often defining moments in our lives.

Today, in the workplace, upward mobility is dependent upon your ability to demonstrate that you are capable of leading *before* being asked. It is not unusual in today's fast-paced, flexible business world to be given new roles and responsibilities without immediately being given the title that goes along with it. In reality, leadership in your life and in your workplace is an internal quality that will determine how far and how fast you are able to succeed.

In these pages, we hope that you will find practical, useful information on how to unlock the leadership skills and abilities that you never knew you had in the workplace. Whether you've just changed roles, careers or are seeking to excel in a new and more desirable position, we trust that you will find this book instantly and widely applicable. After all, your work situation will always be a small factor in your ability to lead; leadership is an internal ability that every person wields in a unique and powerful way. You owe it to yourself and to the world to unlock that potential.

CHAPTER 1: WHAT LEADERSHIP IS AND WHAT IT ISNT

You might have a vague, working definition of leadership, but what is it that makes an individual a great leader? Even with a strong, general understanding of the term, leadership is often misunderstood amidst all of the ideas that are associated with it. Before coming up with a strong definition and understanding of leadership, it would be beneficial to deconstruct some popular misconceptions surrounding the word.

Five Significant Misconceptions Surrounding Leadership:

1. A Great Leader must have a Great Title
Canadian author and leadership speaker, Robin S. Sharma, has this to say about the importance of a leadership title:

"Leadership is not about a title or a designation. It's about impact, influence and inspiration. Impact involves getting results, influence is about spreading the passion you have for your work, and you have to inspire teammates and customers."

There are plenty of CEOs and executive officers who lean too much on their titles to inspire others. We all know, or have at least heard of, the mean and degrading boss. Does that person inspire their team to be the best that they can be? Probably not.

Great leaders bring great ideas to the table, no matter where they are in a company. Seniority and a lofty title do carry a certain amount of weight within a company, but oftentimes, in order to be promoted or to gain a title, you need to demonstrate the leadership skills and abilities required to earn that title.

2. Leaders Must Be Extroverted
Extroversion and introversion take a lot more credit for a person's abilities than they are due. While many great leaders are extroverted, some of the most famous leaders in history were known introverts. People like Abraham Lincoln and Albert Einstein, to name a few, truly valued their introverted tendencies. Leadership involves a certain amount of external obligations, but strong leadership in whatever form requires an ability to produce well thought out solutions, supreme focus and concentration, and openness to constructive feedback and new ideas. All of these are areas in which introverts excel. Instead of leaning on a personality type as an excuse for lacking leadership skills, remind yourself that being a strong

leader is much more dependent upon the action that you take than it is on the type of person that you are.

3. There is Ever Only One Leader

This is not to say that having too many leaders is an impossibility, but most people tend to consider themselves either *the* leader, or a follower. Yet in today's flexible and demanding working environment, there is almost always room for someone to step in and improve their immediate surroundings. Be wary of organizations that do not delegate tasks or responsibilities; these are the marks of a company burdened by trust issues and top-heavy infrastructure.

More and more companies are adopting a leadership strategy that supports the workers who contribute more, resulting in overall more productive and happier workplaces. Stepping up and taking ownership of an idea or project should never be punished, as it alleviates the hardships and burdens of running the company from everyone involved. There are many instances in which leadership calls for immediate and close-quarters response. How could a CEO respond to a complaining customer in one of hundreds of branches as the situation unfolds? The responsibility falls to a branch manager, or a supervisor, but what if they're on break or off-site? Do not let the opportunity to prove yourself fall to the wayside, always be willing to step in and take control of a situation yourself, just be sure to follow the proper chain of command and only step up when you feel that it is appropriate. In this example, a CEO should always trust someone else to solve the immediate problem, and this is true for any circumstance in which you have the ability to influence a situation positively.

4. Leaders Need to Be in Powerful, Prestigious Positions.

Most likely, your CEO gets paid considerably more than you do. It's normal, but that doesn't mean that your CEO is a greedy, power hungry individual. Most followers think poorly of leaders who abuse their power, even in a prideful way. A true leader is not motivated by positions of power, or of great wealth. Good leaders are passionate about what they do, and most likely, it is how they got to be where they are in the first place. Do not believe that leadership is in any way tied to the accrual of wealth or the pride of power, because more likely than not, leaders with these qualities are less respectable and less appreciated.

5. There is No Difference Between Leadership and Management

Contrary to popular belief, these two terms are not interchangeable. They are considerably different from one another, and require a considerably different subset of skills in order to perform well.

Management is interested in *how* to make something happen. They are the ones who delegate responsibility, who plan and coach people through the situations that they need to get through. In short, managers are people who follow through with the logistical or practical means of achieving a certain goal. That frees leaders up to perform their job.

Leadership is all about *why* something should be pursued. While it is true that a leader is often called to take on managerial roles, the true goal of a leader should be to examine from a more abstract perspective the reason that a task should be carried out. They give direction by inspiring vision, by empowering the people around them to pursue a common goal, and they should not tie themselves up with the practical and logistical systems that managers are responsible for.

Successful business owner, author, and educator, Stephen Covey, has this to say about the difference between management and leadership:

"Management is efficiency in climbing the ladder of success; leadership determines whether the ladder is leaning against the right wall."

Leadership: A Threefold Definition
It is difficult to pin down a concise definition of what leadership denotes. After all, we've already established that it encompasses a wide breadth of meaning. In order to come up with a strong definition of leadership and what it means to be a leader, we will need to factor in the most important elements of what leadership entails.

We've already looked at a quote by Robin Sharma in which he identifies three major components to leadership, what he calls "impact, influence, and inspiration." These three entities, along with their respective definitions, according to Sharma, touch on the fabric of what many great leaders identify as the most important elements of leadership. In essence, a good leader should fulfill the following three statements:

1. A Good Leader should Maximize Team Effort
Leaders should have a strong impact on their followers, and should be most interested in getting everyone onboard to quickly and effectively complete the task at hand. Producing results is about more than getting to the end of a project, it is about the care, effort, time, and quality of work put necessary to making sure that the final product is as polished and professional as possible. By fostering a team

environment where every member wants to work, and wants to work well, a good leader can boost the overall brand or quality of a company from the inside.

2. A Good Leader should Move the Team in a Common Direction

Leaders are the ones with vision, who see the possibilities and direction of the company and exert the social influence necessary to move the entire team in that direction. Without a team that believes in what it is doing, or worse, a team that doesn't know what direction it is moving, how can they move towards achieving a common interest? It is up to a strong leader to ensure that a team believes in and is moving in the direction that the company desires to go.

3. A Good Leader should Inspire the Best in the People Around Them

In order to maximize efforts and move a team in a common direction, a leader should be able to inspire the best out of the people around them. This is the attribute that separates strong leaders from figureheads. By merit of a title or through fear, anyone can force others to do their job. But only true, strong leaders can encourage their team-members to truly be the best that they can be, thereby encouraging the best quality of work from them. Even more, a strong leader can influence customers and shape their community through their values and passions. Unlike fear mongering, micromanaging bosses, strong leaders draw out only the best in others, and make them want to strive to succeed.

Leadership is a Skill
With this definition of leadership, we can clearly see that a leader is something unique, defined apart from managers and other authority figures. Leadership qualities are internal skills made external, in the sense that they are centered on their goals in a way that enables others to become moved in a common direction.

We have yet to discuss one of the last major misconceptions about leaders: are they born, or made? Forbes magazine has published an article on the question, and contributor, Erika Anderson, believes that, "most folks who start out with a modicum of innate leadership capability can actually become very good, even great leaders." In other words, while there are some who are or may be born with an innate ability to lead, and there are also some who may never possess the skills necessary to lead, almost everyone falls somewhere in between these two extremes, and everyone has the capacity to develop leadership.

This classifies leadership as a skill, that is, something that can be refined, improved upon, and learned through practice and effort. We are going to ask and answer another question: how you can immediately begin honing your skills as a leader.

CHAPTER 2: IS LEADERSHIP RIGHT FOR YOU?

Leadership is often seen as a daunting task, and rightly so. There is a fair amount of hard work, dedication, and responsibility in every leadership role, no matter how small. There will always be obstacles, challenges, and setbacks that get in your way. At the end of the day, leadership can be a reward in and of itself. Few leaders would condemn their positions of leadership, and almost all agree that the benefits of being in a leadership position far outweigh the consequences. Here is a list of some of the most attractive aspects of taking on a leadership role:

Responsibility
It is difficult to pinpoint exactly what is so alluring about responsibility. For the underprepared, it can cause anxiety and become a burden for the individual with a severe fear of failure. Yet for those who are ready and confident in their leadership role, responsibility can build strong feelings of satisfaction and freedom in the workplace. A business is essentially the product of its leadership, so to be on the side of the business that directly influences company culture or profitability, can be a feeling unlike anything else in a task-oriented, follower's role. If you feel bored or unhappy at work, that may be a

strong indicator that you desire the weight and responsibility of a leadership position.

Goals

Anyone who has ever participated on a sports team knows that when the team scores a goal, the whole team celebrates. And for those who know the feeling of being the person to score the goal, the sensation of doing so borderlines euphoria. The same holds true for companies, and especially true for the leaders who are directly responsible for setting and moving the team towards a specific goal. In the business world, achievement and reaching goals is in and of itself a win. Victory comes in the form of offering superior quality services or products than local or global competitors, and in this sense, becoming the person who determines the course and actions towards victory is an immensely attractive aspect of leadership.

People

Motivating people to be their best and seeing the fulfillment that comes from a strong work ethic is another great motivator for people considering putting themselves in a leadership position. Many leaders value the positive, driven attitudes of their coworkers and employees, especially when that dedication is a direct result of strong leadership. Many people seek or need guidance in order to achieve, and a good leader will both set high goals for a person, and work with them to get them to achieve that goal. This is how a company grows, by growing its people and helping them to redefine their own abilities and aspirations. Many of the greatest leaders in history were motivated by the feeling of knowing that the people around them experienced growth and achievement as a direct result of their encouragement, motivation, and influence.

Building Something
Leadership is about building up, whether that be a brand new model from the ground up, or building on an existing structure. A leader directly contributes and adds to company culture, a company's direction, its values, and all of the interpersonal relationships that drive the company forward. Being able to claim ownership over even a small facet of your company is a huge motivator for people. This is particularly true for businesses that are breaking away from the traditional 9-5 model. Many start-ups and small businesses are transitioning into work environments that are built around team-building activities; stress relieving games, team bonding, and other company cultures that are largely inspired by the voices of the employees themselves.

Ripple Effect

The impact of a strong leader usually extends far beyond that leader's immediate sphere of influence, whether they know it or not. A leader who is able to inspire the people immediately around them to be their best and to maximize their efforts usually enables those people directly influenced to pass the same vision and drive to the people around them. Leaders like Steve Jobs have a transformative power in their leadership style, one that extends beyond their product, beyond their company, and some would go insofar as to say that their influence shapes the culture of their historical moment.

Passion
All of the aspects of leadership that we have discussed come from a place of internal passion and drive for what it is that the leader is doing. At a certain point, all other factors in the workplace melt away against the fact that a leader is allowed to be truly passionate. The nature of the work often takes second place to the joy of being a leader. In fact, most of the factors on this list would be enough for people to find fulfillment and satisfaction in simply being a leader. Passion surpasses any satisfaction that comes from pay, benefits, or bonuses. The pleasure of being able to come into work everyday with excitement, creativity, vision, and energy is perhaps the greatest of all motivators for today's leaders.

Should You Choose Leadership?
At the end of the day, the question of leadership comes down to motivation. We have already established that leadership is not a title or a power that is given; it is a power that comes from an internal drive to innovate, to inspire, and to succeed.

Your motivation must be a desire to bring out the best in others, by the weight of responsibility, by moving people to achieve goals, by building people and companies up, or any of the items on this list, then you should be reaching for a leadership role within your workplace. If you are someone who enjoys micromanaging, who does not trust the people around you, it's not too late to change course. Leadership is open to anyone who is open to a positive, meaningful change in his or her surroundings and in themselves. Scottish novelist, John Buchan, has this to say about the motivating power of leadership: *"The task of leadership is not to put greatness into humanity, but to elicit it, for the greatness is already there."*

CHAPTER 3: APPROACHING A NEW LEADERSHIP ROLE

There are many preparatory steps you can take to prepare yourself for becoming a leader. Most people find the idea of stepping into a leadership position daunting and intimidating. That being said, with the right philosophical foundations, and a strong understanding of how to approach leadership, the act of becoming a leader and leading the people around you to the best of your abilities can be natural and exciting. To begin, let's take a look at two terms that will help anyone to better approach a new role in leadership.

Introspection
As we have already established, true leadership is a largely internal process. It involves making peace with yourself, and becoming confident enough in yourself to inspire and motivate the people around you. Introspection refers to the process of internal reflection and the gaining of self-knowledge. It is a never-ending process of analyzing and understanding your strengths, while also acknowledging and addressing your weaknesses. The process of introspection helps you to formulate and understand your natural style of leadership, allowing you to step back from your own immediate reactions in order to

see whether or not your actions and motivations are in the best interests of the people around you.

To be clear, introspection is not a self-absorbed or narcissistic endeavor. The goal of preparing yourself for a leadership position should always first and foremost be about understanding the way you think and act. All of your past experiences and roles have a part to play in how you will approach leadership: if you hated your condescending boss, then you can shape a kinder and more encouraging way to respond to the people under your command. Use this process to anticipate and prepare for the demands of leadership, and figure out how all of your life experiences have shaped you into the person that you are today. In truth, it is the sum of those experiences and the attitude that you carry towards the world around you that will determine your leadership style and the extent to which that style will be successful in the workplace.

Furthermore, introspection does not end when you become a leader. It is equally critical to the continued success of your leadership endeavors. Constantly assessing and reassessing your actions, motivations, and outcomes is the only way to ensure you are staying on the correct path, and it is the only way to be able to know when the time has come to alter course. In a way, leaders are obligated to serve both the company and the employees under their influence. Listening to constructive criticism, being open-minded to new ideas and change, and setting healthy goals with positive communication are all areas of strong leadership that require times of introspection.

Consider this story as a testament to the power of introspection: The George Washington University School of Business appointed, Doug Guthrie, as dean in 2010 in order to solve a serious budget problem. The school was severely underfunded, and turned to Guthrie's leadership skills and experience to help get the school back on track. Guthrie drastically changed the direction of the school, and managed to properly fund and budget the school within two years by implementing and controlling a new model of his own design. Though he had achieved a certain end, he realized that by keeping other faculty and colleagues at arm's length and powering through with his own ideas, he had lost their support and trust. Unfortunately, Guthrie was removed from his position as dean, which shocked many of the students and faculty members who supported the changes in direction that Guthrie had been taking. As it so happens, the administration did not feel included in Guthrie's actions, nor did they feel that they could trust him to move the school forward. Guthrie later reflected that while he does stand by his decisions, the lack of trust created by his personal actions was a failure on his part to listen to and consider opponents of his budget plan. In this case, introspection could have led him down a much different path.

For this reason, introspection is one of the most beneficial tools that a leader can utilize. You should regularly use it to remain humble, and analyze every action that you take, every step of the way. Never fail to consider the complexity and needs of the people around you, as these issues will often set you back more than organizational or logistical issues. That being said, introspection is limited to the experiences that you already have. Let's look at another term that can be used to build experience and strengthen a leader through action.

Outsight
Many first-time parents describe a transition from the time that their child is born, to the time in which they actually feel and act like parents. To be sure, parenting is one of the most challenging and rewarding forms of leadership. In short, they describe the transformation as being initially clueless, afraid, tired, and constantly trying new things and pretending to be the parents that they want to be. Most emulate their own parents, recalling things that worked when they were young, and experimenting with new techniques. All new parents turn to others for advice, listening at every

opportunity to what they could be doing better. After fumbling through parenthood for a few weeks, they suddenly find themselves in the midst of parenthood, and doing a pretty good job.

If that sounds like an allegory for leadership, it certainly is. There is a certain extent to which changing your mentality and using introspection can alter your actions in leadership, but there is equally as much to be said about the process of trying new techniques and acting like the leader you eventually want to be. This is a process called outsight, and it is becoming more popular among leaders who do not lean as heavily on purely introspective processes.

Herminia Ibarra, a Professor of Leadership at INSEAD and former Harvard Business School faculty member, believes that outsight is the key to success for new and emerging leaders. If your leadership style is only built on your past experiences and internal thought processes, then how will you look forward to the problems that currently do not exist? The business world of today demands flexibility, innovative thinking, and creative solutions, and Ibarra argues that in order to meet the demands of these constantly evolving environments, we must change our actions before we change our thoughts. By creating new solutions and constantly searching out new methodologies, you will have more raw material to work with during times of introspection. And if something works particularly well, you will be free to simply go with it and process the solution as it unfolds. This active, as opposed to reactive, style of leadership is critical in today's business world.

Acting the Part of a Leader
In order to act like the leader you want to become, Ibarra lists three necessary components of your environment that you should constantly seek to redefine:

1. The Job
Nowadays, leadership roles rarely come with official promotions and raises. More likely than not, you will need to apply yourself and lead in new and different ways from within the position you currently hold. Even though the title can lead to more clarity and more ability from within a leadership role, you should be able to adapt and redefine your position within your role as it evolves. The demand of leadership from the ground level of a company only increases as the company grows, and in order to make serious moves from your current position, you will need to regularly demonstrate the leadership qualities that make you the most competitive candidate for the official promotion or change in role. If you find yourself in a role that is changing often, it is no leap of logic to conclude that you should be able to change too.

One of the best ways to initiate this change is to bring other people on board with both your new tasks, and the tasks that you are familiar with being assigned. Delegating and motivating groups of people to complete the tasks assigned to a team is a great way to put yourself out there as someone who is willing to act like and be the leader. If your moves lead to increased productivity across your team as a whole, you could attract the attention of the people above you, and maneuver yourself into an entirely new realm of action. Always redefine your position and be making transitions in your thoughts and actions.

2. Your Network
Inspiration and change should be as motivated by the people around you as it is in your own mind. Allowing others to help spark change empowers them, while also causing them to view you in a change maker or leadership role. Again, acting the part is half of the job. By allowing a constantly evolving network to shape and influence your decisions, you will be empowered to become the leader that others seek, even as they begin to see you that way. Over time, you will feel less and less strange in the way you approach and set expectations for others. This is the beginning of formulating an identity in leadership, and it is a process that will occur naturally over time. As you receive constructive criticism or a congratulations,

and as people seek you out for your opinions and instructions, you will suddenly find yourself no longer acting. You will simply have become the leader you felt like you were pretending to be.

3. Yourself
If you feel stunted in your abilities as a leader, the most likely cause will almost always be yourself. Inspiring others implies that we ourselves are constantly inspired, and in order to define yourself as a leader in your ordinary, everyday circumstances, you will need to constantly redefine and reassess who you are in the grand scheme of things.

This is a difficult process; most people are naturally opposed to taking action that disrupts the stability and security of our personal identity. In that sense, the person who will consistently stand in the way of new, bold, and positive change is yourself. If there is an option in which the worst-case scenario is simply change for the sake of making a change, you should be open to taking it. New experiences are the foundation for growth, and failing to redefining yourself would be to assume that you are already the absolute best version of yourself that you can be. If that is the case, then there should be no need to make any changes in your life. Since that is untrue for all of us, be brave enough to step out into new, unfamiliar territory. Be courageous enough to face scary and intimidating situations, to try new things, and see where those opportunities will go. Only then will you be able to chase new dreams, bigger dreams, and opportunities that would never have presented themselves had you stayed comfortably and quietly in the places that you have always been.

Leadership is a Process
That path to becoming a strong leader is ill defined, and is never an easy or straightforward path. It is something you will need to embark upon and figure out for yourself. As you redefine yourself and your surroundings, you will pick up key elements of knowledge and insight that will contribute to how you approach problems and goals throughout your entire life. You will fail, sometimes brilliantly, but if the ones who failed never tried again, our civilization would scarcely be recognizable.

Do not fall into discouragement when things don't go immediately as planned, when you encounter a setback, and never be frustrated at the pace of improvement. You will not become the world's greatest leader in a day, or a year, or maybe ever. But if you set out today to become a slightly better leader, a slightly better person, than you were the day before, then every day will be marked by growth and progress, until you are somewhere you never dreamed of being. Keep pushing onward, and always remember to root yourself in introspection and outsight, so that the foundation for your leadership style is strong and adaptable to the world around you.

CHAPTER 4: BUILDING LEADERSHIP SKILLS IN THE WORKPLACE

Leadership does not allow for shortcuts or cutting corners, but there are definitely ways you can ensure that you are on the right path to discovering your own leadership style and methods. Before trying the techniques we are about to go through, remind yourself that there will be good days, and there will be bad days. There will be times in which you experience large amounts of growth and improvement, and there will be times where you feel stuck and unsure of yourself. Always do your best to remain positive, and remember there is no right or wrong way to go about defining yourself as a leader.

As we look at different ways to build your leadership skills, treat every item as a guide, and not as a checklist. If something doesn't work as well for you at first, continue to push forward in it, and if you find that you really excel at other items on the list, make those items the foundation of your leadership style.

Expanding Your Network
Networking is one of the most important abilities for a leader to have. Your network refers to the people around you, who are within your immediate sphere of influence, who you can rely on to help you or give you

advice when the going gets tough. No one should ever try to lead alone, especially anyone who wants to grow as a leader. Leadership involves building healthy, constructive relationships of people who will push you forward, who will keep you accountable to your own actions, and who will provide you with the criticism and feedback necessary for you to grow in your role. Always be willing to meet and interact with new people, even (or especially) if it is in a one-on-one or small group setting, and before long you will find yourself with a circle of confidants and acquaintances who will benefit from a constructive and mutual business relationship.

Showing Enthusiasm
Leadership is all about energy, and showing enthusiasm can be one of the most important traits that you can take into work every day, even if it is not sincere or natural. No one will be motivated to work harder or contribute more if you do not set the tone and set an example for what strong, enthusiastic work ethic should look like. No one can go every single day with a high energy, enthusiastic attitude, but on days when you don't feel at your best, you should still maintain a positive and perseverant presence. The ability to hold your emotions in check, even if you are going through a considerably emotionally stressful time in your life, will prove vital to your abilities to

move people in a common direction day in and day out. Never allow problems to fester or grow due to an unwillingness to face them, and never turn away from conflict situations that arise. There are many challenges and setbacks that leaders face in their week-to-week endeavors, and the emotional stability required to approach and handle them all is critical to the success of your team or business.

Being Authentic
Yes, we did just suggest that you should be enthusiastic even if you don't feel like it, but there is a difference between authenticity and always putting your best foot forward. You may be having a bad day, but you should genuinely want your company to succeed underneath whatever turmoil you may be experiencing. You should always believe in the vision you set for yourself and for others. Moreover, in order to become more genuine and dependable, practice these four important and practical guidelines:

1. *Get to Know Your Team and the People You Lead*
The people that come in day in and day out to work with you, or work for you, have their own lives, cares, concerns, struggles, and passions. You owe it to them and to yourself to get to know them, at least on a professional level. You do not need to be best friends with everyone you work with, and to a certain extent, you should not pursue that. You should always listen,

and always remember to check in with your employees to make sure they are happy, healthy, and motivated to reach their goals and the goals of the company. Building up your team should be among your highest priorities, as the potential for great success and growth lies within each and every one of them. Allow your team to surprise you, and never underestimate their potential when they strive individually and collaborate together. By building up their confidence and being actively involved in who they are as people, you will earn their loyalty and motivation to be the best that they can be each day that they come in to work.

2. Act Ethically, Responsibly, and Always Keep Your Word

The fastest way to lose someone's trust or confidence is to break your word, or behave in a way that would have negative repercussions for anyone else. If you set rules for the workplace, be absolutely sure you can adhere to them and set a proper example. If you promise someone something, be sure to follow through and fulfill your commitment. Being the person who sets the tone of a work environment means those who are watching and emulating you will magnify your negative qualities. For that reason, you should never make unethical decisions, slack off while others are working, or act as though you are not accountable for your own actions.

3. Take Ownership for Mistakes and Share the Credit

Team morale is dependent on a constructive and positive environment. You will want your employees to take risks and reach for creative, out of the box solutions, to project goals and challenges. In order to ensure your team is working at its best, you should always take the blame for mistakes. No one will see you as any lesser. In fact, taking the blame for mistakes that are not your fault will be praised as a noble and a noteworthy feat. When things go well and a team effort produces positive results, be sure to share the credit for the achievement as much as you can. The more you can make your team feel valued, the more they will respect you, and that leads to greater productivity and overall happier teammates and employees.

4. Stand by Your Decisions

There should always be a fair amount of forethought and preparation before making a decision, but once you make your decision, you should always stand by it. There will be times when you will doubt yourself or doubt the direction of your decision, but by changing your mind or expressing insecurity, you threaten the chances that the goal will be achieved. Unless something happens or evidence arises that shows your decision is overtly wrong and detrimental to the company, you should look for creative solutions to challenges and remain steadfast in your decision-making abilities.

Always Be Learning
Situations are going to continually present themselves to you in new and unique ways. Technologies exist today that did not exist ten years ago, and next year, there will be new and complex factors at play in the business world that do not necessarily exist today. We live in a constantly expanding and changing environment, so do not allow yourself to be hardheaded and set on one specific way of doing things. Always be open to learning new modes of business, and always look for ways to adapt and improve your method of doing business. Be aware of the constantly changing tides of social media, advertisement, and the practical realities surrounding the rapidly globalizing market. If something arises that you do not understand, you should learn about it as fast as you can, using any opportunity available to you.

Delegate
A good way to understand delegation would be to understand the importance of trusting your team to do good work without you leaning over their shoulders.

Micromanaging is one of the most detrimental traits a leader can have, and will often compromise a team's ability to perform or function well. Learn to delegate and trust your team members with key aspects of a project, and leave the logistics to managers, so that you can keep the company's goals and visions in sight.

Help Others Succeed

In leadership, you do not succeed unless your team succeeds. Getting wrapped up in personal ambition will often cause you to stumble and lose sight of the direction that your team should be heading. Create the best possible environment for your team members to succeed and be open to coaching others towards their own successes. If you help others to achieve, they will in turn follow you in pursuing your goals.

Learning From Other Leaders

You will never have time to explore every avenue or every option available to you. Sometimes, you may find yourself wondering what the outcome could have been had you chosen a different path. More likely than not, other leaders in a similar position as you will have succeeded or failed in their endeavors in a way which could improve your own understanding of how best to lead in your situation. Within a team setting, you should feel comfortable enabling others to take the lead, that way you can observe the ways in which certain ideas or certain energies benefit or negatively impact the company as a whole. Every time someone is allowed to bring their own ideas to the table, they will gain a sense of ownership over the project, and that will inspire a whole new level of production in them. Learn to work with other leaders, be it from within your own company, or from external organizations, and learn how you can best capture their attitudes or energies towards leading.

Inspire and Motivate
Instead of becoming wrapped up in office politics or small issues, always try to think of what you are doing in a larger scale than the people around you. If you are selling a service, think of ways in which that service is meaningful, and share your thoughts with the team. If it is a product, ask yourself how your product benefits the lives of the people around you. These ideas bolster your sense of pride in your work, which naturally filters out into inspirational and motivational leadership qualities. If all you do is show up, put in a day's work, then leave, you will not command the inspiring quality that makes so many leaders respectable and motivational. Try to focus less on the achievement of goals, and more on why the goal should be achieved in the first place. That way, you will not be subject to discouragement. You will always be focused on the vision, and not consumed by the challenges of getting there.

Develop a Strong Executive Presence
You do not need to be a ranking level executive officer in order to carry an executive presence. As you begin to take lead, the people will feel your presence in the workplace, and it is up to you to make sure your presence is one that promotes healthy, positive outcomes.

Executive presence is hard to pinpoint, and can be hard to monitor, as it is essentially the perception that others have about your personhood as a leader. To others, you may appear to be someone who carries authority, who is trustworthy and open, or who should be paid attention to when they are speaking. This presence is about image; it is about how straight you stand and how confident the look in your eyes is. This is an area of leadership that some people come into naturally, but for those who do not immediately radiate strength and authority, there are many ways to improve your executive presence. It all boils down to your self-confidence, in fact, a vast majority of your executive presence will stem naturally from how confident you are in yourself and in your abilities. In order to boost the perception others have of you, and in order to improve the executive presence you carry among your peers, pay attention to these three areas of your interpersonal actions:

1. Communication

There is a finesse to communicating as a leader that can be difficult for many people to master. There are many things to avoid; you do not want to be boring, overloading, drawn out, monotonous, unsteady, or unclear. Always try to be clear and concise when communicating your desires and instructions. Be careful not to wander off into confusing or ambiguous tangents, as this will lead to complications and messy situations either immediately or later down the road. In short, you should be comfortable communicating everything you believe will be necessary to the achievement of your goals and the goals of the company. Sometimes you will make a misstep in conversation, or something that you say may strike someone in a way other than the way that you meant it. Simply take note of the mistake, correct it, and work to make sure that you come across as clearly and confidently as you can in your interactions.

This applies to presentations and speaking to groups of people, as well. By treating a presentation as you would any other conversation, you will naturally begin to improve your communication skills as a whole. Public speaking is one of the most prevalent fears in the world, but by learning to talk to a group of people as you would an individual, a lot of that fear will naturally dissipate. Allow for questions, engage your audience, and never become hostile or antagonistic. Your insecurities may intensify when speaking to a group, but keep in mind that each person in the audience considers themselves simply one person listening to what their leader is telling them. The group is not a single body intent on driving out your insecurities, so be confident and communicate in universal, simple statements.

2. Appearance
Keep in mind that as a leader, people are looking at you differently than they might look at one another. Problems in personal appearance will be magnified and may jeopardize your executive presence. As a leader, there are important aspects of your physical appearance that you should never fail to be aware of.

You should always, first and foremost, be well groomed and well dressed. While these standards may differ slightly for men and women, the goal should always be to appear professionally and conservatively attractive. Since attraction is often a standard of beauty, suffice to say these standards are subjective. Men should be clean-shaven or have tasteful, well-groomed facial hair, should have clean nails, and should wear tasteful, ironed clothes. Women should choose tactful, non-distracting clothing and accessories. Unfortunately, beauty standards are considerably harsher towards women than they are to men, so no matter what you believe about beauty standards, remember the goal of your appearance should always be to command the most respect and authority from the people looking at you. Different work environments will have different standards for what this means, for example, you probably shouldn't wear an expensive suit to a non-profit center for the homeless. Be tasteful and aware of what your environment calls for, and always practice good hygiene.

Your posture will also play a large role in determining the amount of executive presence that you carry. You will not carry the same amount of authority if you slouch or constantly fidget. Be strong, upright, and focused on anything and everything that demands your attention.

3. *Gravitas*
This term refers to a certain weight or substance that you will carry wherever you go. It might be translated to your "importance" in a room of peers. In order to build this sense of weight and get people to take you seriously, consider the way you act around others. Gravitas surrounds people who act confidently, who observe situations with a commanding eye, and who is generally more aware of themselves and their surroundings than others around them.

Never listen to the fears and insecurities that creep behind your convictions and thoughts. Beating yourself up is perhaps the most negative of all possible traits that you could have as a leader. By always looking forward, acting like you know what you are talking about, refraining from apologizing or constantly proving yourself, you will naturally build self-confidence and build the confidence that others have in you. Remain calm and always be prepared to learn more from times of challenge and setback. In situations that demand your attention, get used to observing and processing information actively. That way, you can be the one who says what has not yet been said, or participate in a way that resolves or contributes to the solution of a problem.

Ultimately, you need every component in this chapter to build your gravitas. It is somewhat elusive, and depends on things that we don't often think about. Remembering names, smelling good, avoiding "um" and "uh," awkward poses, dirty or stained clothes, and all manner of small personal factors will contribute to the weight that people feel when you are present in a room.

How to Become Unstuck
Once again, all of the items in this list of ways to build leadership skills are guidelines. They are meant to help you on your journey to becoming the best leader

you can be, but sometimes, you will feel stuck. Always remember that the feeling of being stuck is an illusion, and in that sense, identifying it as quickly as you can is always the first step to ridding yourself of it.

Though you may feel uncomfortable or immobile in your leadership position, don't fall into thinking you can rationalize your way out of it. If you find that something you've been doing successfully is no longer working, realize that it is probably because your circumstance has changed, not you. Once you realize this, you will be able to attack a new solution, and trade your out-of-date ideas or methods for new, innovative, and constructive approaches. In any circumstance where you find yourself suddenly feeling stuck or trapped, experiment and take risks that you never have before, and before long you will have shaken up your circumstances enough to take off in a progressive and positive direction.

The most profound and simple piece of advice that you can remember when feeling stuck is this: do something. It doesn't matter what your next move is, or if it is going to be successful or not, just make a move and be prepared to adapt and face the outcome. Staying put is the only way to ensure that you continue to feel stuck, so make the change first, then deal with the consequences. If you truly are reaching a plateau, or stagnating, then the odds are in your favor that a new direction will be healthy and beneficial. There will always be people around you to counsel you if things become especially unclear, so come to a decision and pursue a new course of action before you drive yourself and the people around you into a standstill.

CHAPTER 5: LEADERSHIP STYLES

We've spent a fair amount of time looking at ways to help you develop your own leadership style, and most likely, your preferred strategies and methods will shape a style of leadership that is unique to you. Still, we want to take the time to explore some established modes of leadership and identify a wide breadth of skills that make a good leader. It is important to remember to be flexible to your surroundings, and for that reason, you will always need to adapt your leadership style. Before identifying today's major leadership styles, let's take a look at a theory of leadership that you can use to constantly evolve within your leadership role.

Theory of Situational Leadership
Dr. Paul Hersey, founder of the Center for Leadership Studies, developed a model of leadership theory with the foundational premise that there is no single, best style of leadership. Rather, good leadership depends on the intelligent application of diverse skill sets and strategies in the workplace. Strong leaders should be able to adapt their resources to meet the needs of the team and the task at hand, and in that sense, situational leadership is an ongoing process of assessment, action, reassessment, and so on.

Hersey's theory creates an awareness of a team member's maturity, skill set, experience, and motivational energy in order to complete a task or project. A leader can then respond with a certain level of social or emotional support, and provide the right amount of direction or trust to ensure that projects are completed in a healthy, efficient manner.

The theory of situational leadership identifies four major steps that a situational leader should take in any given scenario. By remembering to follow these four steps, you should find yourself switching between leadership styles without always realizing it. This means that you are becoming a strong and adaptable leader in your workplace. These are the four steps that Hersey lists for the process of selecting the best leadership style for any given situation:

1. Diagnose
Take a step back and break down situations in your mind as they occur. Take the time to understand how the circumstances might be impacting the people around you, and how that might change the way you are able to influence them.

2. Adapt
Change your behavior to match the tone and demands of the circumstance. Always seek to respond in a way

that is appropriate to how everyone around you is feeling.

3. Interact
Take communicative measures and touch base with the people around you. Get them to understand and support any changes in direction, and make sure that they feel comfortable and motivated to fulfill new or different roles.

4. Advance
Always create the feeling of moving forward. This will help you and your team bond over the feeling of accomplishment, and will allow you to greatly solidify and increase the influence you have in adverse or challenging situations.

The situational leadership model was developed in the 60s and early 70s, but it is still widely accepted and practiced in the business world today. Given the ever-changing nature of the business world today, this is an extraordinary testament to the theory's universality and strength. That being said, there are numerous leadership styles that are appropriately employed today, and you need to know how and when to use them. We will explore six of these styles so you can easily transition between them when your circumstances change.

Goleman's Six Styles of Leadership

Daniel Goleman, author of the *New York Times* bestselling novel *Emotional Intelligence*, conducted research of more than 3,000 business executives and published an article in the *Harvard Business Review* magazine outlining what he identifies to be the six most prevalent leadership styles and directions in the world today. They are:

1. The Pacesetting Leader

This style is all about setting the example of what you want out of your team. It is most applicable to smaller, self-directed teams that excel on their own motivational strength and autonomy. By working harder, smarter, and more passionately than the individuals around you, your team will naturally strive to keep up with you and match your performance output. In the short-term, this style can boost productivity immensely, and create short periods of strong feelings of accomplishment.

Pacesetting suffers in the long-term, and is not a good idea for teams where feedback, patience, training, direction, or adjustment is regularly called for. When used too much, it can cause severe burnout, underperformance, and a group of stressed and discouraged team members. Use sparingly for extraordinary short-term results, and only use if you are confident that your team will be able to motivate and drive themselves.

2. The Authoritative Leader

A leader using this style can unite aimless or confused teams by inspiring in every team member a strong and clear vision of the common goal. The team can then produce their own methods for reaching that goal. Often, this style is most beneficial to creative teams who need vision, not guidance. It encourages these types of team members to come up with creative solutions and builds energy with every successful new idea. This style produces the most positive work environment when properly employed, and relieves the leader of taking on a cumbersome managerial and task-oriented role.

The only pitfall of this style concerns team members who may feel they have a better vision or goal for the team in mind. Sometimes, they may even be right, so if you choose to adopt an authoritative leadership style, you need to be sure that your vision is built with care, passion, and sense at its core.

3. The Affiliate Leader

This style of leadership is built upon encouraging team members through praise or emotional support, which creates a positive company culture and an inclusive, healthy sense of belonging in the workplace. It is particularly useful during periods of stress, overwork, or trauma in the workplace. Affiliate leadership is second only to the authoritative leader in the positive impact that it can have on a community. It will not guarantee productivity boosts or high achievement, but it will always create a happier, healthier team dynamic.

Using affiliate leadership too much, or exclusively, can lead to complacency, or a lack of motivation. Similarly, team members who regularly make mistakes and are not given constructive criticism or feedback will continue to make the same mistakes over and over again. This style is best paired with another, result-oriented style.

4. The Coaching Leader
This leadership style is structured around providing training and building up the technical skills necessary for a strong and independent team. It assists in setting and achieving goals for other team members, challenging them to achieve more, and balancing action with opportunities to learn and expand skill sets. While this role is built around communication and listening to the needs of team members, it is ultimately the leader's role to give assignments and set the expectation.

Don't expect immediate results if you use this style, especially if you give challenging assignments outside of a team member's immediate area of expertise. You must also ensure that you are the most proficient in your area of instruction, which is impossible to do in a diverse work environment. While you may not see immediate results, over time you will find that overall productivity significantly increases, and your team members will be less afraid of taking risks and rising to challenges.

5. The Coercive Leader

This was once the most commonly used style of leadership, but has fallen in standing as the business world demands more inclusive teamwork and multifaceted problem-solving abilities. This style, also known as the autocratic leader, is about one thing: control. It can be used in times of crises, where a new and absolute sense of direction needs to be dictated by one person. It can also be used on an individual team member who responds poorly to other leadership styles, or if the individual needs particular direction and order.

Most of the time, this leadership style will fail to create a positive, healthy work environment. When used over a group, it will only alienate members and prevent creativity. If you seek a rigid, tightly managed office, then this leadership style will certainly get you there, but more often than not it will cause others to label you as insecure and untrustworthy.

6. The Democratic Leader
This style incorporates the opinions of the team members into problem-solving and creative thinking, leading to a strong feeling of ownership over ideas and open, constructive lines of communication. The leader is free to frame and direct projects, while the team contributes where invited. This style is also known as participative leadership, and allows team members to take a more active role within creating company culture. It is a great way to observe changing environments, and will allow you to see the way that your team interacts and thinks through problems together.

The only downside to using this style frequently is that it is slow and often creates new problems, even if it solves others. If an immediate change is required or a time sensitive deadline is approaching, it's wiser to switch to another, more immediate style of leadership. That being side, with freedom of time, and especially in an R&D capacity, this style of leadership can lay a long-lasting and positive foundation for change and team morale.

CONCLUSION

Taken all together, this eBook should help you to realize your fullest potential as a leader, no matter where you are in life. The skills and methods taught here are applicable to your leadership abilities as a parent, friend, or community member. Whether you feel like you were born to lead, or feel as though you may never be cut out for leadership, there will be times where you will be called to lead. The moments where you step up to the challenge and take action will define you in the eyes of others, and more importantly, to yourself.

Always remember that leadership is a process. There are no easy, well-defined paths on the road to becoming a great leader, and the only common piece of advice that you will find throughout history is this: be true to yourself. You may not lead like General Ulysses, or like Martin Luther King Jr., but you will lead like **You**, and that is the greatest contribution that you can choose to make to the world around you.

THANKS FOR READING

We really hope you enjoyed this book. If you found this material helpful feel free to share it with friends. You can also help others find it by leaving a review where you purchased the book. Your feedback will help us continue to write books you love.

The Smart Reads library is growing by the day! Make sure and check out the other wonderful books in our catalog. We would love to hear which books are your favorite.

Visit:
www.smartreads.co/freebooks
to receive Smart Reads books for FREE

Check us out on Instagram:
www.instagram.com/smart_readers
@smart_readers

Don't forget your 2 FREE audiobooks.
Use this link www.audibletrial.com/Travis to claim your 2 FREE Books.

SMART READS ORIGINS

Smart Reads was born out of the desire to find the best information fast without having to wade through the sheer volume of fluff available online. Smart Reads combs through massive amounts of knowledge compiles the best into quick to read books on a variety of subjects.

We consider ourselves Smart Readers, not dummies. We know reading is smart. We're self taught. We like to learn a TON about a WIDE variety of topics. We have developed a love for books and we find intelligence attractive.

We found that each new topic we tried to learn about started with the challenge of finding the pieces of the puzzle that mattered most. It becomes a treasure hunt rather than an education.

Smart Reads wants to find the best of the best information for you. To condense it into a package that you can consume in an hour or less. So you can read more books about more topics in less time.

OUR MISSION

Smart Reads aims to accelerate the availability of useful information and will publish a high quality book on every major topic on amazon.

Smart Reads hopes to remove barriers to sharing by taking the copyright off everything we publish and donating it to the public domain. We hope other publishers and authors will follow our example.

Our goal is to donate $1,000,000 or more by 2020 to build over 2,000 schools by giving 5% of our net profit to Pencils of Promise.

We want to restore forests around the globe by planting a tree for every 10 physical books we sell and hope to plant over 100,000 trees by 2020.

Doesn't it feel good knowing that by educating yourself you are helping the world be a better place? We think so too...

Thanks for helping us help the world. You Smart Reader you...

Travis and the Smart Reads Team

WHY I STARTED SMART READS

Every time I wanted to learn about something new I'd have to buy 20 books on the topic and spend way too long sorting through them and reading them all until I arrived at the big picture. Until I had enough perspectives to know who was just guessing, who was uninformed and who had stumbled upon something remarkable.

I wished someone else could just go in and figure that out for me and tell me what matters. That's how smart reads was born. I want smart reads to be a company that does all that research up front. Sorts through all the content that is available on each topic and pulls out the most up to date complete understanding, then have people smarter than me package the best wisdom in an easy to understand way in the least amount of words possible.

For example, I got a new puppy so I wanted to learn about dog training. I bought 14 different books about dog training and by the time I got through the first 5 and finally started getting the big picture on the best way to train my puppy she had grown up into a dog.

Yeah she's well behaved. She doesn't poop in the house. I can get her to sit and come when I call. But what if someone else went in and read all those books for me, found the underlying themes and picked out the best information that would give me the big picture and get me right to the point. And I'd only have to read one book instead of 15.

That would be amazing. I would save time. And maybe my dog would be rolling over, cleaning up after my kids and doing the dishes by now. That my friend, is the reason I started smart reads. Because I wanted a company I can trust to deliver me the best information in an easy to understand way that I can digest in under an hour. Because dog training is one of many subjects I want to master.

The quicker I can learn a wide variety of topics the sooner that information can begin playing a role in shaping my future. And none of us knows how long that future will be. So why not do everything we can to make the best of it and consume a ton of knowledge. And I figured all the better if I can also make a positive difference in the world.

That's why we're also building schools, planting trees and challenging ideas about copyright's place in today's world. Because as a company we have to be doing everything we can to support the ecosystem that gives us all these beautiful places to read our books. Thanks for reading.

Travis

Customers Who Bought This Book Also Bought

Develop Self-Discipline: Daily Habit to Make Self Confidence and Will Power Automatic

Self-Esteem Supercharger: Build Self Worth and Find Your Inner Confidence

Success Principles: Techniques for Positive Thinking, Self-Love and Developing a Powerful Mindset

Passive Income: Do What You Want When You Want and Make Money While You Sleep

Neuro Linguistic Programming: NLP Techniques for Hypnosis, Mind Control, Human Behavior, Relationships, Confidence

Credit Repair Guide: How to Fix Credit Score and Remove Negatives From Credit Report

Artificial Intelligence: Understanding A.I. and the Implications of Machine Learning

www.ingramcontent.com/pod-product-compliance
Lightning Source LLC
Chambersburg PA
CBHW051819170526
45167CB00005B/2077